Francis Frith's
WEST SUSSEX

PHOTOGRAPHIC MEMORIES

Francis Frith's

WEST SUSSEX

◆

Nick Channer

FRITH
BOOK Co

First published in the United Kingdom in 2000 by
Frith Book Company Ltd

Hardback Edition 2000
ISBN 1-85937-148-5

Paperback Edition 2002
ISBN 1-85937-607-x

British Library Cataloguing in Publication Data

Francis Frith's West Sussex
Nick Channer

Frith Book Company Ltd
Frith's Barn, Teffont,
Salisbury, Wiltshire SP3 5QP
Tel: +44 (0) 1722 716 376
Email: info@francisfrith.co.uk
www.francisfrith.co.uk

Printed and bound in Great Britain

Contents

FRANCIS FRITH: *Victorian Pioneer*

FRANCIS FRITH, Victorian founder of the world-famous photographic archive, was a complex and fascinating man. A devout Quaker and a highly successful Victorian businessman, he was both philosophic by nature and pioneering in outlook.

By 1855 Francis Frith had already established a wholesale grocery business in Liverpool, and sold it for the astonishing sum of £200,000, which is the equivalent today of over £15,000,000. Now a multi-millionaire, he was able to indulge his passion for travel. As a child he had pored over travel books written by early explorers, and his fancy and imagination had been stirred by family holidays to the sublime mountain regions of Wales and Scotland. 'What a land of spirit-stirring and enriching scenes and places!' he had written. He was to return to these scenes of grandeur in later years to 'recapture the thousands of vivid and tender memories', but with a different purpose. Now in his thirties, and captivated by the new science of photography, Frith set out on a series of pioneering journeys to the Nile regions that occupied him from 1856 until 1860.

INTRIGUE AND ADVENTURE

He took with him on his travels a specially-designed wicker carriage that acted as both dark-room and sleeping chamber. These far-flung journeys were packed with intrigue and adventure. In his life story, written when he was sixty-three, Frith tells of being held captive by bandits, and of fighting 'an awful midnight battle to the very point of surrender with a deadly pack of hungry, wild dogs'. Sporting flowing Arab costume, Frith arrived at Akaba by camel seventy years before Lawrence, where he encountered 'desert princes and rival sheikhs, blazing with jewel-hilted swords'.

During these extraordinary adventures he was assiduously exploring the desert regions bordering the Nile and patiently recording the antiquities and peoples with his camera. He was the first photographer to venture beyond the sixth cataract. Africa was still the mysterious 'Dark Continent', and Stanley and Livingstone's historic meeting was a decade into the future. The conditions for picture taking confound belief. He laboured for hours in his wicker dark-room in the sweltering heat of the desert, while the volatile chemicals fizzed dangerously in their trays. Often he was forced to work in remote tombs and caves where conditions

were cooler. Back in London he exhibited his photographs and was 'rapturously cheered' by members of the Royal Society. His reputation as a photographer was made overnight. An eminent modern historian has likened their impact on the population of the time to that on our own generation of the first photographs taken on the surface of the moon.

VENTURE OF A LIFE-TIME

Characteristically, Frith quickly spotted the opportunity to create a new business as a specialist publisher of photographs. He lived in an era of immense and sometimes violent change. For the poor in the early part of Victoria's reign work was a drudge and the hours long, and people had precious little free time to enjoy themselves.

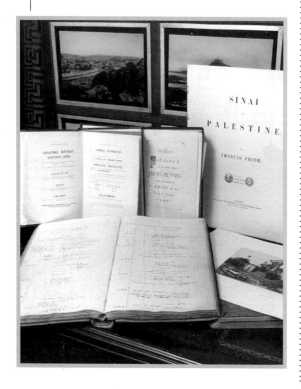

Most had no transport other than a cart or gig at their disposal, and had not travelled far beyond the boundaries of their own town or village. However, by the 1870s, the railways had threaded their way across the country, and Bank Holidays and half-day Saturdays had been made obligatory by Act of Parliament. All of a sudden the ordinary working man and his family were able to enjoy days out and see a little more of the world.

With characteristic business acumen, Francis Frith foresaw that these new tourists would enjoy having souvenirs to commemorate their days out. In 1860 he married Mary Ann Rosling and set out with the intention of photographing every city, town and village in Britain. For the next thirty years he travelled the country by train and by pony and trap, producing fine photographs of seaside resorts and beauty spots that were keenly bought by millions of Victorians. These prints were painstakingly pasted into family albums and pored over during the dark nights of winter, rekindling precious memories of summer excursions.

THE RISE OF FRITH & CO

Frith's studio was soon supplying retail shops all over the country. To meet the demand he gathered about him a small team of photographers, and published the work of independent artist-photographers of the calibre of Roger Fenton and Francis Bedford. In order to gain some understanding of the scale of Frith's business one only has to look at the catalogue issued by Frith & Co in 1886: it

runs to some 670 pages, listing not only many thousands of views of the British Isles but also many photographs of most European countries, and China, Japan, the USA and Canada – note the sample page shown above from the hand-written *Frith & Co* ledgers detailing pictures taken. By 1890 Frith had created the greatest specialist photographic publishing company in the world, with over 2,000 outlets – more than the combined number that Boots and WH Smith have today! The picture on the right shows the *Frith & Co* display board at Ingleton in the Yorkshire Dales. Beautifully constructed with mahogany frame and gilt inserts, it could display up to a dozen local scenes.

POSTCARD BONANZA

The ever-popular holiday postcard we know today took many years to develop. In 1870 the Post Office issued the first plain cards, with a pre-printed stamp on one face. In 1894 they allowed other publishers' cards to be sent through the mail with an attached adhesive halfpenny stamp. Demand grew rapidly, and in 1895 a new size of postcard

was permitted called the court card, but there was little room for illustration. In 1899, a year after Frith's death, a new card measuring 5.5 x 3.5 inches became the standard format, but it was not until 1902 that the divided back came into being, with address and message on one face and a full-size illustration on the other. *Frith & Co* were in the vanguard of postcard development, and Frith's sons Eustace and Cyril continued their father's monumental task, expanding the number of views offered to the public and recording more and more places in Britain, as the coasts and countryside were opened up to mass travel.

Francis Frith died in 1898 at his villa in Cannes, his great project still growing. The archive he created continued in business for another seventy years. By 1970 it contained over a third of a million pictures of 7,000 cities, towns and villages. The massive photographic record Frith has left to us stands as a living monument to a special and very remarkable man.

Frith's Archive: *A Unique Legacy*

FRANCIS FRITH'S legacy to us today is of immense significance and value, for the magnificent archive of evocative photographs he created provides a unique record of change in 7,000 cities, towns and villages throughout Britain over a century and more. Frith and his fellow studio photographers revisited locations many times down the years to update their views, compiling for us an enthralling and colourful pageant of British life and character.

We tend to think of Frith's sepia views of Britain as nostalgic, for most of us use them to conjure up memories of places in our own lives with which we have family associations. It often makes us forget that to Francis Frith they were records of daily life as it was actually being lived in the cities, towns and

villages of his day. The Victorian age was one of great and often bewildering change for ordinary people, and though the pictures evoke an impression of slower times, life was as busy and hectic as it is today.

We are fortunate that Frith was a photographer of the people, dedicated to recording the minutiae of everyday life. For it is this sheer wealth of visual data, the painstaking chronicle of changes in dress, transport, street layouts, buildings, housing, engineering and landscape that captivates us so much today. His remarkable images offer us a powerful link with the past and with the lives of our ancestors.

TODAY'S TECHNOLOGY

Computers have now made it possible for Frith's many thousands of images to be accessed almost instantly. In the Frith archive today, each photograph is carefully 'digitised' then stored on a CD Rom. Frith archivists can locate a single photograph amongst thousands within seconds. Views can be catalogued and sorted under a variety of categories of place and content to the immediate benefit of researchers. Inexpensive reference prints can be created for them at the touch of a mouse button, and a wide range of books and other printed materials assembled and published for a wider, more general readership - in the next twelve months over a hundred Frith local history titles will be published! The day-to-

See Frith at www.francisfrith.co.uk

day workings of the archive are very different from how they were in Francis Frith's time: imagine the herculean task of sorting through eleven tons of glass negatives as Frith had to do to locate a particular sequence of pictures! Yet the archive still prides itself on maintaining the same high standards of excellence laid down by Francis Frith, including the painstaking cataloguing and indexing of every view.

It is curious to reflect on how the internet now allows researchers in America and elsewhere greater instant access to the archive than Frith himself ever enjoyed. Many thousands of individual views can be called up on screen within seconds on one of the Frith internet sites, enabling people living continents away to revisit the streets of their ancestral home town, or view places in Britain where they have enjoyed holidays. Many overseas researchers welcome the chance to view special theme selections, such as transport, sports, costume and ancient monuments.

We are certain that Francis Frith would have heartily approved of these modern developments, for he himself was always working at the very limits of Victorian photographic technology.

THE VALUE OF THE ARCHIVE TODAY

Because of the benefits brought by the computer, Frith's images are increasingly studied by social historians, by researchers into genealogy and ancestory, by architects, town planners, and by teachers and schoolchildren involved in local history projects. In addition, the archive offers every one of us a unique opportunity to examine the places where we and our families have lived and worked down the years. Immensely successful in Frith's own era, the archive is now, a century and more on, entering a new phase of popularity.

THE PAST IN TUNE WITH THE FUTURE

Historians consider the Francis Frith Collection to be of prime national importance. It is the only archive of its kind remaining in private ownership and has been valued at a million pounds. However, this figure is now rapidly increasing as digital technology enables more and more people around the world to enjoy its benefits.

Francis Frith's archive is now housed in an historic timber barn in the beautiful village of Teffont in Wiltshire. Its founder would not recognize the archive office as it is today. In place of the many thousands of dusty boxes containing glass plate negatives and an all-pervading odour of photographic chemicals, there are now ranks of computer screens. He would be amazed to watch his images travelling round the world at unimaginable speeds through network and internet lines.

The archive's future is both bright and exciting. Francis Frith, with his unshakeable belief in making photographs available to the greatest number of people, would undoubtedly approve of what is being done today with his lifetime's work. His photographs, depicting our shared past, are now bringing pleasure and enlightenment to millions around the world a century and more after his death.

WEST SUSSEX - *an introduction*

THE COUNTY OF West Sussex symbolises the English countryside at its best. Some say it is England. Probably the best way to appreciate its gentle beauty is to explore it on foot - just as that eminent man of letters Hilaire Belloc did one hundred years ago at the beginning of the 20th century. Belloc spent much of his life in Sussex, and years before the county was divided into two, a victim of the detested county boundary changes of 1974, he chose to walk from Robertsbridge in the east to Harting in the west - a journey of some 90 miles. Belloc recorded his impressions of rural Sussex during his odyssey, and many of the landmarks and features associated with his route appear in this book. With their eye for detail and their knack of picking just the right subject, Frith's team of well-respected photographers completed a fascinating illustrated record of the county's towns and villages when they journeyed through West Sussex around the same time as Belloc, and on a number of other occasions in subsequent years.

Frith's team of professionals may not have followed Belloc's example and walked across this part of southern England, but they did the next best thing by photographing it. And there can surely be no finer legacy for future generations than to produce an illustrated social record of what they saw and where they went. Their pictures tell us so much about life as it used to be, revealing in fascinating detail how we have changed and how we continue to evolve. It is impossible to look at Frith's early photographs of Sussex without acknowledging the tide of change that has swept the world in the intervening years.

The scenes in many of the Victorian and Edwardian photographs of West Sussex look much the same today as they did then; yet since the period when those pictures were taken, Britain has undergone enormous upheaval. The horror and brutality of two world wars were unimaginable at the beginning of the 20th century, and yet their ghastly images still haunt us today. Since those dark days, man has landed on the moon, invented the computer and ushered in a modern way of life that both Francis Frith and Hilaire Belloc would undoubtedly find very confusing.

But to what extent has progress influenced the county of West Sussex? Much has changed, and yet much has remained the same in this delightful corner of the country. Parts of the coast have altered beyond recognition since Frith's photographers captured classic seaside scenes at Bognor, Worthing and Littlehampton, and now a chain of urban development extends all the way from Brighton to Chichester. Busy roads and out-of-town superstores have replaced quiet backwaters and unspoiled stretches of coast. Only occasionally is there a glimpse of the Sussex we see portrayed in this book. Away from the sea, Frith's revealing portraits of country villages and small towns provide an endless source of fascination, and here, perhaps, the changes have been fewer and less obvious.

Our village communities are etched into the fabric of our society, reflecting a way of life that is unique throughout the world. West Sussex is blessed with many fine villages and picturesque towns which, in the main, have stood the test of time and remained largely intact. Some have fallen victim to planning blight and seen their boundaries expand in recent years, while others have fought off late 20th-century development, their pride and spirit undented. The village, in particular, is an integral part of the British landscape, and nowhere is that more strongly represented than in West Sussex. These communities have played a key role in shaping our rural heartland and influencing its distinctive character. Many villages are distinguished by those elements that have helped make them a matchless part of our heritage - the church, the local inn, the post office and the community hall among other familiar ingredients. No two communities are the same - each village is highly individual, with its own fascinating history, culture and tradition. Despite school, shop and pub closures, and the fear of an uncertain future, the village remains a unique institution - just as it was in Francis Frith's day.

But it is not the coastline, the towns, or the villages that makes West Sussex unique. It is the magnificent natural landscape of the South Downs that sets this county apart from the rest. Think of West Sussex, and one thinks immediately of those glorious, green hills stretching towards the sea. Designated an Area of Outstanding Natural Beauty, the 90-mile chain of the Downs, wooded in the west, bare and exposed in the east, provides local residents, as well as visitors and holidaymakers, with a perfect natural playground.

During the Victorian and Edwardian eras, when walking was an especially popular pastime, long before the motor car choked our roads and motorways, many people would head for the South Downs to take a bracing hike along the ridge of these hills, their jaunts often accompanied by the faint tang of the sea. Centuries before Frith's photographers began capturing images of West Sussex for posterity, the Romans used this part of the country as a strategic bridgehead for the conquest of Britain, and even today there is evidence of Roman roads extending to London.

Another rural treasure in West Sussex is the Ashdown Forest, which straddles the border with East Sussex and is the largest area of uncultivated land in south-east England. Covering about 20 square miles, and once part of the much larger Wealden Forest, the area is now a mixture of high, open heathland, oak and birch woodland and clumps of pine dotted about this well-wooded sandstone hill region of the High Weald. Ashdown was a Royal Forest for 300 years, and prehistoric man hunted here before the Roman invasion. The Romans successfully established a well-organised iron industry here, and were also responsible for building a road through the forest. However, in the post-Roman Dark Ages, Ashdown was little disturbed by outside influences. Now it is the well-trodden domain of the motorist and city dweller seeking peaceful recreation in the country.

But an overview of West Sussex should also include the county's towns, which are well-represented in this book. Worthing and Littlehampton evolved as fashionable coastal resorts in the days when most British families never strayed beyond these shores for their annual holiday. With their neat public gardens, bracing seafronts and comfortable hotels, these seaside towns drew visitors from far and wide. Inland, West Sussex boasts many charming country towns - Midhurst, Haywards Heath, Pulborough and Petworth among them. Crawley has changed and expanded over the years, and Frith's photographs of quaint old buildings and traffic-free streets seem a far cry from the New Town image of today. At the other end of the county is Chichester, one of Britain's loveliest cathedral cities and possibly the first Roman military city in England. Compare the photographs of Chichester in this book with the reality of today, and one is reassured to see that some features of the city remain permanent, unchanged and timeless.

If I had the time, I would be tempted to travel through West Sussex, much as Hilaire Belloc did all those years ago, and study the changes that have taken place since these photographs were developed. What a fascinating journey that would be. It would not just be an odyssey through one of England's loveliest counties, but a journey through time. No matter what the future holds, the past cannot be denied. And the photographs in this book offer a fascinating insight into the daily pattern of our lives - in both town and country. They create a permanent social record for our children to study and learn from in the years ahead. It is good to know that although much of our world may have changed for good, Frith's photographs of West Sussex evoke special memories and unique images that will never fade.

SELSEY, THE LIFEBOAT HOUSE 1930 83449

ITCHENOR, YACHTS ON THE WATER 1960 146045

Overlooking colourful Chichester Harbour, Itchenor lies at the confluence of the Bosham and Chichester channels of the estuary and was originally named Icenor. Between the 1600s and 1800s, the village played a vital role in the shipbuilding industry. Eventually, any trace of its previous prosperity became submerged beneath the houses and the harbour mud.

EAST WITTERING, THE BEACH 1930 83452

There are two Witterings - East and West. Both villages, which lie at the end of the Selsey peninsula, just a few miles from the historic cathedral city of Chichester, have long been associated with seaside holiday recreation. This photograph captures the spirit of the British at play by the sea; today, the Witterings form part of a continuous ribbon of beachside development.

BOSHAM, THE VILLAGE AND THE CHURCH 1902 48341

Bosham, which lies on the eastern edge of Chichester Harbour, is renowned for its picturesque setting and sturdy Saxon church, which contains an unusual crypt and the grave of one of King Canute's daughters. According to Sussex legend, Bosham is where Canute ordered the waves to recede, though this has been disputed many times over the centuries.

BOSHAM, THE HARBOUR 1903 50912

Bosham, pronounced Bozzam, has a reputation for flooding. The waters rise at flood-tide, reaching the sills of the cottage doors, and over the years television news programmes and local newspapers have carried pictures of motor vehicles stranded in the water. The picturesque cottages and boating activity here have long made this part of Sussex an obvious subject for artists and photographers.

BOSHAM, THE OLD MILL 1903 50921

This old watermill at Bosham has changed a little since this photograph was taken in the early years of the 20th century. Converted to a house, the upper floor now has many more windows, including a dormer window above the weatherboarded section in the middle. Bosham is famous for a saying which suggests that at high tide she is a fine lady, but at low tide, a slut.

SELSEY, THE LIFEBOAT HOUSE 1930 83449

The quiet little seaside town of Selsey was once part of a small island. Today, it is still almost entirely enclosed by water - the English Channel lies to the south-east and south-west, Pagham Harbour to the north-east, and a brook, known as the Broad Rife, to the north-west. The Lifeboat House is now a museum dedicated to the history and development of the R.N.L.I.

SELSEY, HIGH STREET c1960 S91190
During the reign of William the Conqueror, Selsey was a larger town than today, with many important buildings and a cathedral. However, much of it has been engulfed by the sea over the years. The cathedral was built by St Wilfrid, who taught the local townsfolk to fish.

SIDLESHAM, THE VILLAGE c1955 S589003
Dogs are at play in this photograph of a peaceful West Sussex village. Sidlesham sits at the edge of Pagham Harbour, the haunt of redshanks, curlews, grey plovers, ringed plovers and godwits - among other birds. At one time there was a bustling quay here, with ships loading for France. The salty tang of the sea on the wind reminds you that the English Channel is only a stone's throw away.

YAPTON
The Church 1898
The village of Yapton lies between Bognor Regis and Littlehampton. Note the church's jumble of unusual angles and architectural styles. The porch leans forward at an alarming degree, and its roof-ridge projects above the sill of the window above it - an obvious later addition.

BOGNOR REGIS
The Beach 1890
The suffix 'Regis' was added to the name of this seaside town in 1929 after George V spent some weeks recuperating in the area following a major illness. Nearly 150 years earlier, Bognor was the focus of ambitious plans to transform the resort, then only a tiny settlement, into a fashionable watering-place known as Hothamton. Some re-development work went ahead, though the new name never caught on.

YAPTON, THE CHURCH 1898 42567

BOGNOR REGIS, THE BEACH 1890 22626

BOGNOR REGIS
The Beach Hotel 1898 42584

Bognor's Beach Hotel opened in the 1840s and closed in 1963. The town is fondly remembered for its sandy beaches, which are now more shingle than sand. Safe bathing and a host of traditional family attractions made Bognor a popular destination in the great days of British seaside holidays. Queen Victoria referred to the place as 'dear little Bognor'.

BOGNOR REGIS
The Parade and the Pier 1911 63793

On the left is Bognor's pier, one of the town's more familiar features. Constructed in 1865, the structure later became something of a liability and had to be rebuilt in 1910. The new, improved pier included a theatre and arcade. However, the seaward part of it was destroyed by storms in the mid-1960s, and a further section disappeared in 1999.

BOGNOR REGIS, FROM THE PIER 1903 50183

Beyond the line of bathing machines, waves crash against the beach in this turn-of-the-century photograph. Much of the town's architecture dating from this period survives today. Not far from where this picture was taken is a stone which commemorates the opening of this stretch of the seafront in 1899, though the sea air has eroded the writing over the years.

BOGNOR REGIS, HIGH STREET 1890 22633

Here we see Bognor's curving High Street in the days when the internal-combustion engine was in its infancy. Carriages can be seen along the street, and over on the right is a goat cart. On the left is the facade of the Post Office. The High Street is noted for its Arcade shopping centre, which dates back to 1901 and includes ornamental stained glass.

CHICHESTER, WEST STREET 1923 73656

The graceful spire of historic Chichester Cathedral soars above the buildings of West Street. The spire collapsed in 1861 and was rebuilt under the supervision of Sir George Gilbert Scott. Ranging from Norman to Perpendicular in style, this magnificent building includes a shrine to St Richard, Romanesque stone carvings and tapestries by John Piper.

CHICHESTER, THE MARKET CROSS 1890 22617

The intricately-decorated Market Cross is considered to be one of the finest of its kind in the country. It was Bishop Story who made a gift of the cross to the city; he also endowed the Prebendal School in West Street. Note the bookseller and stationer on the left, and the road sweepers standing at the base of the cross.

CHICHESTER
The Market Cross 1892 29983
Situated at the junction of what were originally
Roman roads, and distinguished by its flying
buttresses, the cross is one of the Chichester's
most famous landmarks. Built early in the 16th
century by Bishop Storey, the purpose of the
cross was to provide shelter for traders who came
into the city to sell their wares.

CHICHESTER, EAST STREET 1890 22622
The Market Cross and Chichester Cathedral spire can just be seen in this Victorian photograph. On the left is the Corn Exchange, built in 1830 for local corn auctions. The building later became a theatre, then a cinema which closed in 1980. Today, the front of the old Corn Exchange is a McDonalds restaurant.

BOXGROVE, THE PRIORY 1899 44895
This very well-known Sussex landmark has an air of quiet beauty and dignified charm about it. Built between 1115 and 1220 as a cell of the Abbey of Lessay near Cherbourg, Boxgrove Priory includes a particularly fine chancel among many other striking features. The 15th-century galleries in the transepts are thought to be unique in this country.

COCKING, THE VILLAGE 1906 54385
Local residents used to pronounce it 'Kokkun'. The village is famous for a charming myth which suggests that if the mist in the beechwoods on the nearby Downs rolled westwards towards Cocking, then rain was on the way. Some of the buildings in the village are owned by the Cowdray Estate.

HARTING, THE SHIP INN 1906 54415
Four years before this photograph was taken, the famous writer and poet Hilaire Belloc walked across Sussex from Robertsbridge in the east to Harting in the west. Built of ships' timbers, the 17th-century Ship Inn survives as a traditional local. The sign on the wall reads: 'Good accommodation for cyclists; parties catered for; good stabling; pony and trap for hire'. The writer Anthony Trollope lived here briefly.

AMBERLEY, THE VILLAGE FROM THE CHURCH c1960 A44002

Standing on a plateau overlooking the Arun Valley, Amberley is often described as 'the pearl of Sussex' and 'the loveliest village in Sussex'. The labels are certainly apt, and the village boasts a delightful mix of architectural styles. The setting is very pretty too, with the Downs rising on one side and the Amberley Wild Brooks, a haven for wildlife, on the other.

AMBERLEY, THE CHURCH AND THE CASTLE 1906 56689

Amberley Castle, seen on the right, dates back to Norman times and was strongly fortified in 1377. It was originally the residence of the Bishops of Chichester, though its fate was sealed when the Parliamentarians began to dismantle it during the Civil War. Parts of the castle survive today, having been skilfully converted into an hotel.

AMBERLEY
The Parish Church c1960

Dating mainly from the 13th and 14th centuries, the church at Amberley retains several striking Norman features. Nearby are rows of pretty cottages and ancient, timber-framed buildings with walls of wattle and daub.

ARUNDEL
The Black Rabbit 1898

Overlooking the pretty Arun near Arundel, the Black Rabbit was first licensed in 1804; at that time it was a popular watering-hole for workers digging a new cut of the river. Several years after this photograph was taken, it became a fashionable haunt of Edwardians. Today, the Black Rabbit is popular with riverside walkers and those visiting the nearby wildfowl reserve.

AMBERLEY, THE PARISH CHURCH c1960 A44001

ARUNDEL, THE BLACK RABBIT 1898 42551

ARUNDEL
High Street 1902 48792
The Norfolk Arms can be seen half way up the High Street. The hotel takes its name from the Dukes of Norfolk, formerly the Earls of Arundel, whose principal ancestral home is Arundel Castle. Note the chequerboard design on the gable to the right of the hotel - the pattern signifies that this was once a gunsmith's premises.

ARUNDEL, THE CASTLE AND THE BRIDGE 1928 81374
Full of quaint old Georgian houses and historic buildings, Arundel has long been an obvious destination for tourists and visitors. The great battlemented castle can be seen standing guard over the town; there has been a fortification on this site since the 11th century, though most of the present castle is Victorian. In the foreground is the bridge over the fast-flowing Arun.

ARUNDEL, THE CASTLE AND THE TOWN HALL 1923 73632
There are various family portraits inside the castle, some of them dating back to the Wars of the Roses. The Norfolks have lived at Arundel since the 16th century: according to the plaque at the bottom of the High Street, 'Since William rose and Harold fell, There have been Earls at Arundel'

BIGNOR, THE ROMAN VILLA C1965 B505027

The villa, one of the largest in Britain, was discovered by a ploughman in 1811. On show to the public are various mosaics, which are considered to be among the finest in the country. The entire estate may have extended to about 200 acres, confirming that an important and very wealthy person resided here - perhaps the Roman equivalent of an English aristocrat.

DUNCTON, THE VILLAGE 1912 64897

The village of Duncton lies to the north of the South Downs. The scene looks quiet enough in this early 20th-century photograph, but today the village has to cope with the noise of the A285 Petworth to Chichester road. Lime kilns were once an integral part of the countryside surrounding Duncton.

GOODWOOD HOUSE
The Racecourse 1904 52291

One of Britain's most famous racecourses, Goodwood enjoys a superb position amid magnificent beechwoods high on the South Downs. For one week every July it becomes 'Glorious Goodwood' when thousands of racegoers come to Sussex to attend one of the most exciting events of the sporting and social calendar.

GOODWOOD HOUSE
The Racecourse 1904 52295

The racecourse opened in 1801 after the Duke of Richmond gave part of his estate, Goodwood Park, to establish a track where members of the Goodwood Hunt Club and officers of the Sussex Militia could attend meetings. Towards the end of the 19th century it acquired a rather unfortunate reputation when the rector of nearby Singleton protested over the noisy behaviour of racegoers.

GRAFFHAM, THE VILLAGE c1955 G195006
Graffham is known in the area for its long, winding main street. To the south of the village lies some of the most spectacular downland in Sussex - a popular haunt of walkers and outdoor enthusiasts. Note the pram in the front garden, and the picturesque stone cottages. The bus stop on the left is a reminder of the urgent need for public transport in rural areas.

FITTLEWORTH, UPPER STREET 1921 70081
Here we see picturesque timber-framed cottages in the centre of Fittleworth, to the south-east of Petworth. A mile or so to the north of the village is a house where Edward Elgar spent his summers between 1917 and 1921. It was here that he wrote his best-known chamber music, including the String Quartet.

FITTLEWORTH, THE MILL 1908 60184
This picture depicts an old watermill in a picturesque setting just outside the village. Over to the right is a horse-drawn mowing machine. When this photograph was taken, Fittleworth had its own railway station nearby, and something like one thousand gallons of milk a day, produced at local farms, were loaded onto trains here.

FITTLEWORTH, FROM LEA HILL 1908 60179
Fittleworth became a popular haunt of artists and writers over the years. The village's close proximity to the River Rother also made it popular with anglers. The bridge probably dates back to at least the 17th century, and the old coaching inn was originally two 14th-century cottages.

PARHAM, THE HOUSE 1894 34403

This magnificent Elizabethan mansion is one of the county's gems. The wonderful setting, deer park and views of the South Downs enhance its beauty. Little has changed here since Tudor times. The foundation stone was laid by the young son of Robert Palmer, who was granted the estate in 1577. Today the house and grounds are open to the public.

PARHAM, THE CHURCH 1894 34404

The church, which is dedicated to St Peter, was built in 1545 and almost rebuilt between 1800 and 1820. Up until this time, Parham was very isolated and inaccessible with no proper roads to enable visitors to reach the estate. The small village around the church all but disappeared at the end of the 18th century, helping to maintain the privacy of Parham House.

BURPHAM, THE CHURCH 1898 42557
Only a stone's throw from the historic settlement of Arundel, the village of Burpham is a gem of a place. Pronounced 'Burfam', the village is famous for its 12th-century church, which contains a leper's window through which the wretched victims of this terrible disease were blessed by the priest who remained inside the church. One author summed up Burpham's beauty by saying: 'seldom is a village so delightfully situated, even in Sussex'.

ANGMERING-ON-SEA, THE FORESHORE c1960 A327064
This is a very pleasant Sussex village, with various narrow roads leading down to the coast. The houses, largely grouped in private estates, are part of a chain of residential developments extending roughly from Littlehampton to Worthing. The shingle and sandy beach enhances this sedate retirement community.

ANGMERING, THE CHURCH 1899 42570

ANGMERING
The Church 1899
The church of St Margaret lies at Angmering, not to be confused with neighbouring Angmering-on-Sea. The church is thought to have been restored by the local squire with the proceeds of a win on the Derby.

FERRING
Church Lane c1960
Despite encroaching development, there is still the hint of a quaint old village here at Ferring. The pebble and sandy beach provides views along the coast to Worthing pier; just a short distance inland are the grassy slopes of Highdown Hill, which has long been a popular recreational area for families.

FERRING, CHURCH LANE c1960 F130020

RUSTINGTON
The Church and the Lychgate c1960
Another of Sussex's seaside villages, Rustington boasts a few flint-walled cottages and a medieval church. The north face of the sturdy church tower bears an old clock, though it has been here for less than one hundred years. It originally belonged to Great Bedwyn church in Wiltshire before the churchwardens consigned it to a scrap heap. Fortunately, it was rescued and eventually moved to Rustington.

◆

LITTLEHAMPTON
South Terrace 1890
Littlehampton was a thriving port during the Middle Ages, when stone from Normandy was landed here in order to construct many of the county's churches and castles. Much later it became a fashionable seaside resort, its seafront and neighbouring streets lined with handsome Georgian and Victorian villas.

RUSTINGTON, THE CHURCH AND THE LYCHGATE c1960 R81089R

LITTLEHAMPTON, SOUTH TERRACE 1890 22665

LITTLEHAMPTON
High Street 1892 29970
Not much of the old town survives on the east bank of the River Arun. During the Victorian era the streets of Littlehampton were pleasantly quiet - not unlike the pedestrianised centres of many of our towns today. The shops in this photograph no doubt attracted plenty of custom, but it was Littlehampton's coastal setting that really made the town fashionable.

LITTLEHAMPTON
The Beach 1898 42574

Littlehampton's beach is crowded with trippers. Not surprisingly, everyone in this photograph is fully dressed. During the prim Victorian era, to discard even one item of clothing would have been unthinkable. Nearby is a popular area known as The Green, which lies between the town and the sea.

BYWORTH, THE VILLAGE 1906 54367
Only a mile or so from Petworth, the village of Byworth typifies the rural community in this Edwardian photograph.
The picture shows children playing outside rows of timber-framed cottages, and adults intrigued by the prospect
of being photographed.

PETWORTH, LOMBARD STREET 1900 44979
Cobbled Lombard Street is a narrow thoroughfare. This turn-of-the-century picture shows that it was just wide enough to accommodate the traffic of that period. These days, not surprisingly, Lombard Street is pedestrianised. St Mary's parish church dates back to the 14th century, though it was completely rebuilt in 1827.

PETWORTH
East Street 1906 54362

The timber-framed buildings on the left of the street can still be seen today. Just visible by the parish church is the town's distinctive lamp standard designed by Sir Charles Barry, who was responsible for the Houses of Parliament. The lamp standard is a noted landmark in the town, standing at the point where North Street and East Street meet.

PETWORTH, NORTH STREET 1908 60173
Edwardian children pose obligingly in this charming photograph of Petworth. The spire of St Mary's church soars above the town, and to the right is the boundary wall of Petworth Park, the great mansion built by the Duke of Somerset towards the end of the 17th century. The wall is an incredible 13 miles long, enclosing a beautiful park of 2,000 acres.

TILLINGTON, THE VILLAGE 1912 64898
The village has a timeless feel about it. Near the church lies a quaint old pub known as the Horseguards Inn. It is
thought to have been named after the regiment billeted in nearby Petworth Park during the Napoleonic Wars.

TILLINGTON, THE CHURCH 1912 64899
The coronet design on the tower of All Hallows Church is the only one of its kind in Sussex, and rarely found throughout the country. The early 19th-century design is distinguished by flying buttresses at the four corners, meeting in a finial and forming a Scots crown. The architect is not known.

MIDHURST, NORTH STREET 1921 70084

North Street leads out of the town in the direction of Cowdray Park, with which the town is most closely associated. The part 16th-century Angel Hotel and the Midhurst branch of Barclays Bank are still there, as is the Clock House opposite, which today houses offices. The distinctive clock, seen high above the street, no longer works.

MIDHURST, WEST STREET 1931 83759

At the bottom of West Street lies the 15th-century Spread Eagle Hotel, one of the most famous inns in Sussex. Hilaire Belloc regarded it as 'the oldest and most revered of all the prime inns of the world'.

MIDHURST
North Street 1906 54370
The novelist H G Wells attended school at Midhurst.
'I found something very agreeable and picturesque in
its clean, cobbled streets', he wrote, 'its odd turnings
and abrupt corners, and in the pleasant park that
crowds up one side of the town'.

MIDHURST, KING EDWARD VII SANATORIUM 1907 58337
Situated a mile or so from Midhurst, the King Edward VII Sanatorium was conceived in 1901, the year before the King's coronation, 'for the care of educated persons of limited means who were suffering from pulmonary tuberculosis'. The sanatorium was opened by Edward VII in 1906. Today it is a private hospital.

HENLEY AND BLACKDOWN 1928 81398
Situated up towards the Surrey border, Henley and nearby Blackdown lie in some of the loveliest countryside in West Sussex. It is hardly surprising that this corner of the county was photographed by Frith & Co. Tennyson built his second home at Blackdown, which, at 919 feet, is the highest point in Sussex.

FERNHURST, THE VILLAGE 1908 59672
Fernhurst lies due north of Midhurst in rolling, wooded border country near the Surrey town of Haslemere. George Bernard Shaw used to attend meetings of the Fabian Society at a house in the village. Fernhurst is closely associated with the Sussex ironworks industry.

NORTHCHAPEL, THE VILLAGE 1902 48368
The village name used to be spelt as two separate words - North Chapel. When the roads became negotiable, a brick-built toll house was constructed here. It ceased to operate in 1871, at the time when most toll roads were abolished.

LOXWOOD, THE ONSLOW ARMS AND THE RIVER C1955 L304010

LOXWOOD
The Onslow Arms and the River c1955
The Onslow Arms in Loxwood stands close to the Wey and Arun Junction Canal, which was opened in 1816. The canal was intended to link the two rivers to form a continuous waterway from London to Littlehampton, but the railway age killed it off and it closed in 1871. Canal restoration work has taken place in more recent years.

RUDGWICK
The King's Head c1955
The village of Rudgwick stands hard by the Surrey border, its church literally just a few yards from the county boundary. The King's Head bears the sign 'United Ales & Stout - Wines & Spirits'. Before the Beeching axe fell, trains stopped at Rudgwick, on the line between Horsham and Guildford.

RUDGWICK, THE KING'S HEAD C1955 R305009

STOPHAM, THE BRIDGE 1914 66928
Stopham Bridge has long been considered one of the finest and most striking of medieval bridges in the country. Dating back to 1309 and rebuilt in 1403, the bridge is now preserved. Six of the arches are original; however, the central one was raised in 1822 to allow barges to pass through.

STOPHAM, THE BRIDGE 1932 85391
The narrow bridge stands at the confluence of the Rivers Rother and Arun, and replaces a former Anglo-Saxon structure built of wood. A bypass, built in recent years, has relieved the problem of traffic congestion here. The ancient White Hart inn is seen on the opposite bank.

PULBOROUGH, THE CHURCH AND THE WAR MEMORIAL 1921 70064

In common with all lychgates, Pulborough's ivy-covered, 14th-century churchyard gateway was originally built to provide shelter and a resting place for coffins prior to the funeral service. The church is mainly Perpendicular in style, and includes a sizeable 12th-century font. The war memorial stands proudly to the left of the lychgate.

PULBOROUGH, CLEMENT'S BRIDGE 1906 56746

Along the southern boundary of Pulborough lies the River Arun, popular with Edwardian fishermen and boating enthusiasts. The river has always been a key focal point here, and is noted for its Pulborough eel. The Roman Stane Street crossed the Arun at this point and was strongly defended during the Occupation.

COOLHAM, THE HIGH STREET c1955 C424011
The village of Coolham is probably best known for a lovely old house known as the 'Blue Idol'. The house dates from the time of the Armada in 1588, and was originally a Friends' Meeting House. The Selsey Arms Inn, seen on the left in this photograph, is still in business, though the garage opposite, with the familiar petrol pumps, is now closed.

WISBOROUGH GREEN, THE VILLAGE 1896 38176
A spacious green lies at the heart of this charming Sussex village. The church lies on rising ground, and has a distinctive, off-centre tower. The sails of the windmill, seen in the background, were removed some years ago.

BILLINGSHURST, SOUTH STREET 1909 62164

One of the larger villages of Sussex, Billingshurst may get its name from the Saxon 'Billings', or perhaps from the Roman engineer Belinus who was responsible for Stane Street, the Roman road linking London with Chichester. Stane Street enters London at Billingsgate, famous, of course, for its market.

BILLINGSHURST, EAST STREET 1923 74914

Frith & Co captured this same view of Billingshurst sixteen years earlier in 1907, and apart from several trees growing by the side wall of the shop on the right, nothing seems to have changed in the intervening years.

BILLINGSHURST, TEN STEPS 1907 58203

The heavy broach spire of Billingshurst Church rises above the town. The church was enlarged and restored in 1866, though some evidence of its Early English character survives intact. The 'Ten Steps' lead up to the church entrance, though more had been added by the time this photograph was taken.

WORTHING, MARINE PARADE 1890 22677

The largest seaside town in West Sussex, Worthing began to grow as a fashionable resort towards the end of the 18th century. Prior to that it had been little more than a settlement of fishing cottages down by the beach, below the village of Broadwater. It was Princess Amelia who helped put the place on the map by taking a holiday here in 1797.

WORTHING, THE PIER 1921 71445

A classic photograph depicting the quintessential British coastal resort, with Worthing pier in the background and the ornate bandstand in the foreground. Dozens of deckchairs can be seen either side of it, creating a timeless seaside picture. Much rarer today is the sight of women pushing prams.

WORTHING

South Street 1895 35075

This photograph of South Street shows the premises of the London and County Banking Company on the left. One hundred or so years earlier, South Street was a lane just wide enough for two coaches to pass. There is plenty of activity in this Victorian photograph; note the scaffolding on the right and the ladder propped against the side of the town hall.

WORTHING
South Street 1899 43956
The imposing Italianate town hall, occupying a fine
position overlooking South Street, was opened in 1835
and enlarged in 1847. The building was eventually
demolished in 1968 and replaced by a modern
shopping development.

SOMPTING, THE VILLAGE c1955 S148007
Over the years, Sompting has expanded in all directions and is now almost part of Worthing and neighbouring Lancing. The Saxon church is a well-known local landmark, with a distinctive and very unusual cap on the tower known as a 'Rhenish Helm'. This design is quite common in the Rhineland.

BROADWATER, THE VILLAGE 1906 56718
Now a northern suburb of Worthing, Broadwater was once a small coastal settlement. This Edwardian photograph somehow captures the feel of an English village; note the sign beneath the tree, which points towards Brighton and Shoreham.

LANCING, LANCING COLLEGE c1960 L517038
This stretch of the Sussex coast is probably most closely associated with Lancing College, a famous public school, and its neo-gothic Victorian chapel. The latter was begun by Canon Woodard in 1867 with the intention of complementing the school buildings. Work was eventually completed in 1978 after more than a century.

LANCING, THE COLLEGE 1890 22734
The school and its cathedral-like chapel can be seen from miles away, serving as an established local landmark. The chapel has a vaulted roof of stone and chalk rising to a height of 90 feet. Though the building has received much praise, to some it seems completely at odds with its natural downland surroundings.

LANCING, THE BEACH c1960 L11052

The age-old tradition of pony rides on the sand is captured in this photograph of South Lancing beach. The nearby road has houses either side, which limits public access in places. This part of the Sussex coast was once a favourite haunt of smugglers, with tea and brandy among the booty brought ashore.

FINDON, SOUTH DOWN SHEEP c1955 F131067

This charming Sussex photograph captures a broad sweep of the downs, with hundreds of grazing sheep watched over by the shepherd and his dog. Findon has been synonymous with sheep fairs since the 13th century, when a charter was granted by Henry III.

HIGH SALVINGTON, THE OLD MILL 1919 68994
One of the original 'post and socket' mills, suspended on a post and turned into the wind by means of a tailpole, High Salvington dates back to about 1700 and was the first mill in England to be insured against fire.

WASHINGTON, ST MARY'S CHURCH c1960 W359013
The original church was Norman, but was removed to make way for a larger one built by the Knights Templars. The village lies in the shadow of Chanctonbury Ring, one of the most famous landmarks on the South Downs. Formerly an Iron Age circular rampart and the site of a Romano-British temple, Chanctonbury Ring rises to 783 feet.

STORRINGTON, CHURCH STREET c1960 S210081
Sunlight floods the right-hand side of Church Street in this view of everyday life in a small Sussex town. Hilaire Belloc stopped here on his journey across country from Robertsbridge to Harting in the autumn of 1902. Note the sign 'Ye Olde Forge' half-hidden amid the foliage on the right.

STORRINGTON, VIEW TOWARDS KITHURST 1894 34415
There has been a settlement here since prehistoric times, and Storrington has been a market since 1399. This Victorian photograph depicts the view to the south of Storrington, looking towards the downland. The famous South Downs Way long-distance trail runs along the top.

WEST CHILTINGTON, THE CROSSROADS c1955 W360007
Someone once commented that 'if West Chiltington church was in Italy, people would make pilgrimages to see it'. The church is certainly worth a visit, as is the village itself. This mid-1950s photograph shows the centre of West Chiltington, with the village grocer and the Queen's Head pub seen on the right.

STEYNING

High Street 1914 67056

Steyning was a prosperous little town before the
Roman Occupation. Legend suggests that St Cuthman
helped to establish Steyning in the 8th century. Until
about the middle of the 14th century, the town was
also a port of some note, but by then the sea had
begun to recede, leaving the harbour inaccessible to
shipping and the river little more than a stream.

STEYNING, THE VILLAGE 1914 67059

The centre of Steyning includes rows of picturesque gabled houses and period buildings. When the harbour closed to shipping, Steyning concentrated its efforts on becoming a market town, holding a market twice a week and a fair twice a year. The church is of note, with a late-Norman font and a 16th-century tower.

BRAMBER, THE CASTLE c1965 B179061

Bramber Castle was built just after the Norman Conquest to defend the vulnerable and exposed coast of Sussex. The castle was held by the de Braose family until 1326, when it passed to Alice de Bohun and then to her eldest son. It was badly attacked by the Roundheads during the Civil War, and now all that remains is this 70 ft-high gateway.

BRAMBER, THE VILLAGE c1955 B179020
The houses of Bramber are varied and picturesque. Some are built of brick or flint, and some are creeper-clad. The village was once an important port on the River Adur. However, large scale silting set in when the sea level dropped and soon the port became redundant through lack of trade.

BRAMBER, THE VILLAGE 1890 22724

This delightful photograph captures the spirit of childhood, with these small children posing for the camera. Rows of neat cottages line the road; not far away, though not visible here, is the timber-framed St Mary's House. This medieval building has the best example of late 15th-century timber framing in Sussex, and contains the unique printed room decorated for the visit of Queen Elizabeth I.

BRAMBER, THE CHURCH 1890 22723
The sturdy church of St Nicholas was originally the castle chapel, and probably dates back to the 11th century. Like the castle, the church was also a casualty of battle; Cromwell's men apparently used it as a gun emplacement, causing serious damage to the nave and tower.

BRAMBER, THE DOWNS C1965 B179048
A glorious patchwork of fields and woodland stretches away under huge Sussex skies. With their summer breezes, endless views and salty tang of the sea, the uncrowded expanses of the South Downs have long been a favourite haunt of writers and artists.

UPPER BEEDING, THE DOWNS c1955 U40043A

The village of Upper Beeding nestles against the hills. Confusingly, Upper Beeding is lower than its namesake Lower Beeding, which lies about 15 miles away near Horsham. North of the village lies the site of Sele Priory, established by William de Braose and now occupied by the vicarage.

UPPER BEEDING, ST PETER'S CHURCH c1955 U40021

The church probably lies on the site of a Saxon church which was replaced by a stone church. The last major rebuilding took place in 1308. The churchyard looks somewhat neglected in this photograph, with the gravestones almost hidden by long grass.

UPPER BEEDING, BY THE BRIDGE c1955 U40003

The Bridge Inn and adjoining Beeding Bridge are well-known local landmarks. The bridge is mentioned in documents dating back to the reign of Henry III, and probably replaces the old Roman ford. The River Adur carves a passage between Upper Beeding and neighbouring Bamber.

POYNINGS, THE VILLAGE c1955 P253052

Poynings is pronounced Punnings locally; the name comes from a family who held the manor here during the Middle Ages. Note the signs for Lyons Cakes outside Stephens' Stores. Nearby is the famous Devil's Dyke, a famous beauty spot and viewpoint where the views stretch for miles in all directions.

FULKING, THE SPRING c1965 F133021

FULKING
The Spring c1965
A spring flows beside the village street in Fulking, and on the side of the wellhouse is this text: 'He sendeth springs into the valley which run among the hills. Oh that men would praise the Lord for His goodness'. The words are displayed on Victorian tiles.

FULKING
From Dyke Hills c1965
The Dyke Hills are the setting for the Devil's Dyke, a spectacular downland combe or cleft which, according to legend, was dug by the Devil in an attempt to flood the area with sea water and thus destroy the churches of the Weald. The Devil's Dyke is 300 feet deep and half a mile long.

FULKING, FROM DYKE HILLS c1965 F133016

SOUTHWICK
The Lighthouse c1960

The striking stone-built lighthouse at Southwick dates back to 1846; though no longer in use, it is still regarded fondly as a local landmark. The lighthouse stands on the north bank of Shoreham Harbour. There are good views of harbour activity from this point.

SHOREHAM
The Bridge 1919

This is the original Norfolk Bridge, an 1833 suspension bridge spanning the River Adur and designed by W Tierney Clarke. The bridge was removed in the 1920s to make way for a new bridge which was eventually replaced in the 1980s. The original bridge had a toll house.

SOUTHWICK, THE LIGHTHOUSE c1960 S477053

SHOREHAM, THE BRIDGE 1919 69000

SHOREHAM
High Street 1919 68996
The Royal George Hotel was demolished in the late
1930s as part of a road widening scheme. The road
was quite narrow at this point, as seen in the picture,
and town planners felt they had no choice but to
remove the hotel. The sign on the upper part of the
building on the left reads 'Suits to Measure'.

CLAYTON, THE JACK AND JILL WINDMILLS c1955 C419021E
The Clayton Windmills were built in the 19th century. Jack, on the left, is a large brick-built tower mill which was worked until the early part of this century. Jill is a timber construction built in nearby Brighton and transported to this site by teams of oxen in 1852.

KEYMER, THE PARISH CHURCH c1960 K127025
Located in the border country between West and East Sussex, Keymer (or Kymer as it used to be known) has been held by some of the country's richest and most influential families over the centuries. The church, which is mainly Victorian, is attached to a Norman apse.

BURGESS HILL, VIEW FROM DITCHLING BEACON c1965 B284161
Now in the care of the National Trust, Ditchling Beacon was one of a chain of fires lit to warn of the Spanish Armada in 1588. Much earlier than that it was a hill fort. One of the region's great landmarks, Ditchling Beacon reaches a height of over 800 feet and is the third highest point on the South Downs.

PYECOMBE, THE PLOUGH c1955 P254007
The village of Pyecombe lies close to a long railway tunnel which passengers on the London to Brighton line will know well. The Clayton Railway Tunnel was the scene of a tragic rail disaster involving three trains in 1861. 23 people were killed and 175 injured. The church at Pyecombe contains a rare lead font.

WEST GRINSTEAD, KNEPP CASTLE C1960 W361010
Designed by Nash in 1809 and rebuilt to look exactly the same after a fire at the beginning of the 20th century, Knepp Castle stands between the villages of West Grinstead and Shipley. In the grounds are Knepp Mill Pond, the largest lake in Sussex, and the remains of William de Braose's castle.

HENFIELD, HIGH ST C1965 H313058
Henfield is a long, straggling village a mile or so to the east of the River Adur. The 19th-century botanist William Borrer once recorded over six thousand different plant species in the garden of his home here. On the left of the High Street are the premises of Henfield Post Office and the National Provincial Bank, now defunct.

WARNHAM, THE VILLAGE 1907 58199
Situated just outside Horsham, the village of Warnham is noted for its large mill pond. Winter skaters used to risk their lives on the thin ice, and fishing from the bridge has long been a popular activity here. Near the village is Field Place, the birthplace of Percy Bysshe Shelley, who was educated here until the age of ten.

SLINFOLD, THE LYCHGATE c1965 S591016
A pretty village with various Georgian houses, Slinfold lies in the countryside to the west of Horsham. The church contains tablets to members of the Cowper family, ancestors of William Cowper, the 18th-century poet. One of the most prominent features in this photograph is the moss-covered roof of the lychgate.

HORSHAM, LONDON ROAD 1891 29719
The absence of traffic makes this stretch of London Road in Horsham seem unusually spacious. In those days children could stand safely in the road and pose for photographs. We may be thankful that modern development in the town has not ruined too much of its original character.

HORSHAM, GENERAL VIEW 1891 29711

The name of this Sussex town was mentioned in a Saxon charter, though for some reason it is not referred to in the Domesday Book. Following the Norman Conquest, it was given to William de Braose, and in 1617 it became a corporate borough with a common seal and elected bailiffs.

HORSHAM, THE CAUSEWAY 1901 58194

Standing out proudly in this photograph of Horsham's most interesting street is Causeway House, a picturesque half-timbered building dating back to the late Tudor period. Of particular note are the unusual semi-circular windows in the two gables. The house contains a local history museum.

HORSHAM
West Street 1898 42851
Note the jumble of architectural styles in this late
Victorian photograph of West Street. Horsham was
originally a centre for the manufacture of horseshoes
and crossbows, which were regularly used during the
Hundred Years' War between 1338-1452.

HORSHAM, THE PARK AND THE SWIMMING POOL 1934 86302

A bustling scene in Horsham Park, close to the railway station, with many people having fun in the town's swimming pool which was later enclosed. There are plans to close the site and build a new complex with swimming pool, gym and other facilities.

HORSHAM, THE TOWN MILL 1891 29722

The coming of the railway made Horsham a natural target for expansion, helping to boost the town's economy. The River Arun runs through Horsham, and is the setting for several mills which have been converted into office development. Horsham's Town Mill is seen in this photograph.

SLAUGHAM, THE VILLAGE c1960 S476018

Pronounced Slaffham, this quiet village lies close to the A23 London to Brighton road. Note the row of houses on the right - a varied mix of stone houses and tile-hung properties. The Lord of the Manor here paid for Slaugham's telephone wires to be concealed underground so as not to spoil the appearance of the village.

CUCKFIELD, HIGH STREET c1965 C426022

Cuckfield, pronounced Cookfield, is a 13th-century village standing on a ridge 400 feet above sea level. There are many notable buildings in the High Street and in South Street. From the 15th-century church, with its famous tower crowned by a tall spire, there are good views towards the Clayton Windmills.

HORSTED KEYNES, WHITE GATES c1960 H359024

HORSTED KEYNES
White Gates c1960

Horsted Keynes, situated on the western edge of the Ashdown Forest, has a green and an assortment of period houses and cottages. The village is probably most famous as the home of the Bluebell Railway, a popular attraction since it came into private ownership in the early 1960s.

ARDINGLY
High Street c1955

Ardingly, pronounced Arding-lie, is situated to the north of Haywards Heath and is famous in Sussex as the setting for Ardingly College. It is also the home of Wakehurst Place, which is administered and maintained by the Royal Botanic Gardens. The garden is often described as one of the most beautiful in England. This photograph shows the village Post Office and an old red telephone box.

ARDINGLY, HIGH STREET c1955 A207036

LINDFIELD, HIGH STREET c1960 L221115

This photograph shows Lindfield's very long, curving main street, which climbs gently towards the unusually tall spire of the mainly 13th-century church. Note the Red Lion on the right, and the Hovis and Humphreys Bakery sign on the left. Lindfield has merged with Haywards Heath to the south over the years.

HAYWARDS HEATH, ST WILFRID'S CHURCH AND THE SCHOOLS c1955 H252001

St Wilfrid's Church dates back to 1865, and contains a stained glass window dedicated to two brothers. Two other brothers who died within two months of one another are also commemorated. Beyond the church lies Muster Green, the site of a Civil War battle. Today, Haywards Heath is a commuter market town, and many of its residents travel daily to work in London.

BURGESS HILL
London Road c1950 B284051
London Road runs north out of Burgess Hill, another of the county's growing commuter towns. The dawning of the railway age helped in no small way to put Burgess Hill on the map, and the Railway Hotel can be seen on the right in this picture. A branch of Barclays Bank lies further down the street on the corner.

CRAWLEY, HIGH STREET 1903 50756
Crawley was originally a village which grew in importance during the coaching era. Much of the older town has gone, but in and around the High Street there are still reminders of Crawley as it used to be. It was designated a 'New Town' in 1947; today it is a sprawling community within easy reach of London and, of course, Gatwick Airport.

CRAWLEY, POST OFFICE ROAD 1907 57792
Post Office Road was originally called New Road. In the days before Crawley acquired 'New Town' status, it was the town's business centre, eventually changing its name to Post Office Road - home, not surprisingly, of the local post office. A cottage hospital and court house also stood here at one time.

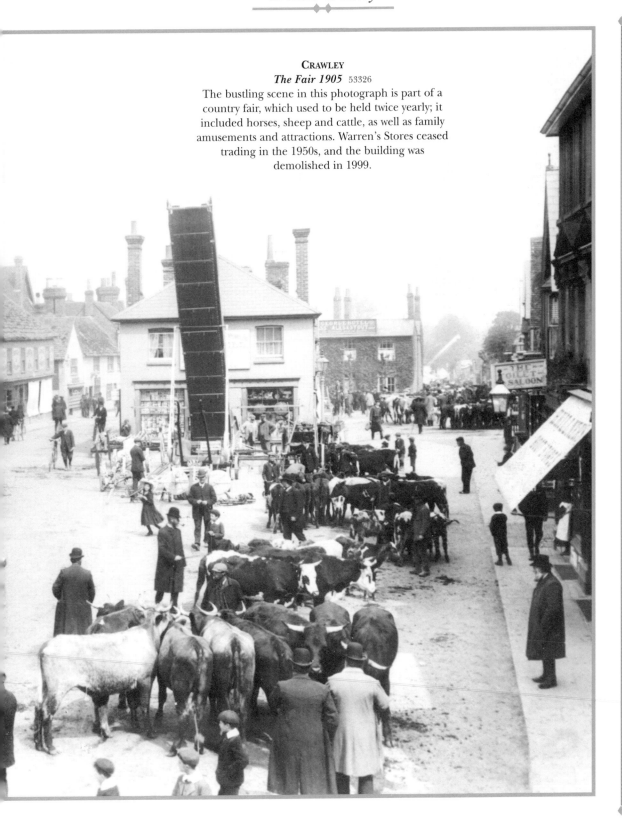

CRAWLEY
The Fair 1905 53326
The bustling scene in this photograph is part of a
country fair, which used to be held twice yearly; it
included horses, sheep and cattle, as well as family
amusements and attractions. Warren's Stores ceased
trading in the 1950s, and the building was
demolished in 1999.

CRAWLEY, OLD HOUSE 1903 50761
The timber-framed cottages seen here were part of Mitchell's Farm, which survived until the 1920s and was the last working farm in Crawley High Street. Over the years the farm buildings have been home to a restaurant and a bank. Today, this is a pub.

WEST HOATHLY, THE VILLAGE 1895 35226
Standing high on a hill with fine Sussex views, West Hoathly is probably best known for its historic church of St Margaret of Antioch. The churchyard consists of six terraces, each one characterised by a retaining wall. The church dates back to 1096; opposite it lies the picturesque 500-year-old Priest House.

IFIELD, THE VILLAGE 1905 53330
Ified was once a typical rural settlement surrounded by open countryside, but these days it is part of Crawley New Town. Note the sign for the Old Plough inn, and the lychgate at the entrance to St Margaret's church. Mark Lemon, the editor of Punch magazine, is buried here.

WORTH, CRAWLEY LANE 1906 55389
Worth lies just to the east of Crawley, beside the busy M23 and not far from bustling Gatwick Airport. None of the villagers seen here could have imagined what changes lay ahead for their community and the surrounding area when they posed for this charming Edwardian photograph.

WORTH, THE LYCHGATE 1906 55392
Often described as one of the finest churches in the country, Worth church is a splendid and historic building. With Saxon foundations and cruciform in shape, the church dates from the 10th or early 11th century. To the right of this photograph is the lychgate, restored in 1956. Much of its timber was retained.

RUSPER, THE VILLAGE AND THE CHURCH 1909 61380
Just visible in this photograph is the church of St Mary Magdalene, which has a large and striking tower. Inside are various old brasses, together with the royal arms of George I. Opposite the church lies the 17th-century Plough Inn, known in the village for its very low beams.

RUSPER, THE VILLAGE 1909 61381
In an age when many village pubs are closing, it is good to know that Rusper still boasts three inns - the Plough, the Royal Oak and the Star. Note the pretty timber-framed cottage on the right.

THREE BRIDGES
Village Centre 1905 53309
Over the years, Three Bridges has been swallowed up by the expanding suburbs of Crawley, but originally it was a very small village. The name pre-dates the railway era, but it was the large station, used by passengers changing from the Portsmouth to the Brighton line, that really put the place on the map. Down the street lies the aptly-named Locomotive pub.

East Grinstead, High Street 1890 27655

Look closely at this photograph, and you can spot the Post Office on the extreme left with the premises of a blind and mattress maker just beyond it. Many of the shops in the High Street are re-fronted timber-framed buildings.

East Grinstead, The Dorset Arms 1904 52900

Situated in East Grinstead's historic High Street, the Dorset Arms stands on the site of a former hostelry known as the New Inn and then the Cat and Ounce. Restoration work took place here in the 18th century, and the tiled roof and dormer windows were added in later years.

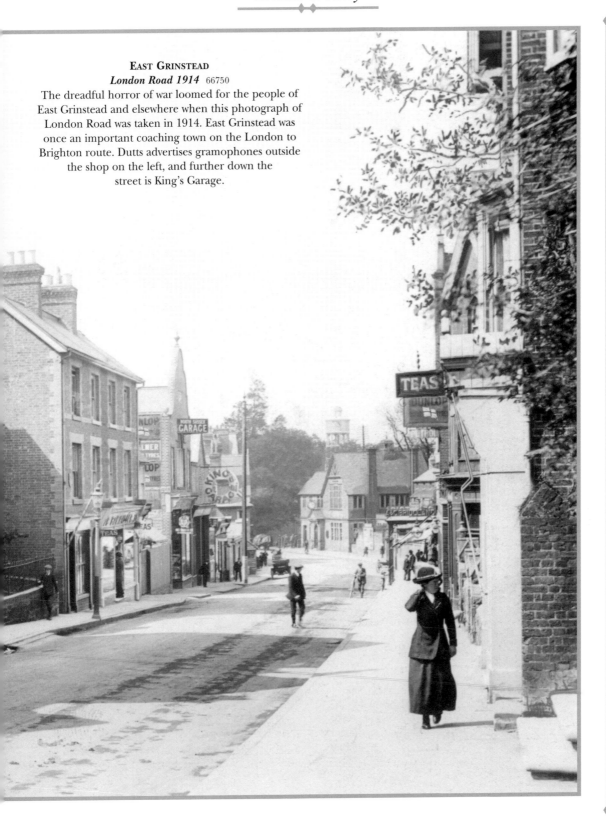

EAST GRINSTEAD
London Road 1914 66750
The dreadful horror of war loomed for the people of
East Grinstead and elsewhere when this photograph of
London Road was taken in 1914. East Grinstead was
once an important coaching town on the London to
Brighton route. Dutts advertises gramophones outside
the shop on the left, and further down the
street is King's Garage.

EAST GRINSTEAD, HERMITAGE LANE 1904 52907
Ten years before this photograph was taken, this part of East Grinstead became known as Hermitage Lane, taking its name from The Hermitage, an 18th-century house demolished in the 1970s. Originally it was known as Hollow Lane and then Brewhouse Lane.

EAST GRINSTEAD, SAINT HILL GREEN 1907 57952
Saint Hill Green lies just outside East Grinstead. The Edwardian children in this picture pose for a group photograph at the road junction. To the left are Felbridge and Hazelden, and to the right is East Grinstead.

Index

Frith Book Co Titles

www.francisfrith.co.uk

The Frith Book Company publishes over 100 new titles each year. A selection of those currently available are listed below. For latest catalogue please contact Frith Book Co.

Town Books 96 pages, approx 100 photos. County and Themed Books 128 pages, approx 150 photos (unless specified). All titles hardback laminated case and jacket except those indicated pb (paperback)

Title	ISBN	Price	Title	ISBN	Price
Amersham, Chesham & Rickmansworth (pb)	1-85937-340-2	£9.99	Derby (pb)	1-85937-367-4	£9.99
Ancient Monuments & Stone Circles	1-85937-143-4	£17.99	Derbyshire (pb)	1-85937-196-5	£9.99
Aylesbury (pb)	1-85937-227-9	£9.99	Devon (pb)	1-85937-297-x	£9.99
Bakewell	1-85937-113-2	£12.99	Dorset (pb)	1-85937-269-4	£9.99
Barnstaple (pb)	1-85937-300-3	£9.99	Dorset Churches	1-85937-172-8	£17.99
Bath (pb)	1-85937419-0	£9.99	Dorset Coast (pb)	1-85937-299-6	£9.99
Bedford (pb)	1-85937-205-8	£9.99	Dorset Living Memories	1-85937-210-4	£14.99
Berkshire (pb)	1-85937-191-4	£9.99	Down the Severn	1-85937-118-3	£14.99
Berkshire Churches	1-85937-170-1	£17.99	Down the Thames (pb)	1-85937-278-3	£9.99
Blackpool (pb)	1-85937-382-8	£9.99	Down the Trent	1-85937-311-9	£14.99
Bognor Regis (pb)	1-85937-431-x	£9.99	Dublin (pb)	1-85937-231-7	£9.99
Bournemouth	1-85937-067-5	£12.99	East Anglia (pb)	1-85937-265-1	£9.99
Bradford (pb)	1-85937-204-x	£9.99	East London	1-85937-080-2	£14.99
Brighton & Hove(pb)	1-85937-192-2	£8.99	East Sussex	1-85937-130-2	£14.99
Bristol (pb)	1-85937-264-3	£9.99	Eastbourne	1-85937-061-6	£12.99
British Life A Century Ago (pb)	1-85937-213-9	£9.99	Edinburgh (pb)	1-85937-193-0	£8.99
Buckinghamshire (pb)	1-85937-200-7	£9.99	England in the 1880s	1-85937-331-3	£17.99
Camberley (pb)	1-85937-222-8	£9.99	English Castles (pb)	1-85937-434-4	£9.99
Cambridge (pb)	1-85937-422-0	£9.99	English Country Houses	1-85937-161-2	£17.99
Cambridgeshire (pb)	1-85937-420-4	£9.99	Essex (pb)	1-85937-270-8	£9.99
Canals & Waterways (pb)	1-85937-291-0	£9.99	Exeter	1-85937-126-4	£12.99
Canterbury Cathedral (pb)	1-85937-179-5	£9.99	Exmoor	1-85937-132-9	£14.99
Cardiff (pb)	1-85937-093-4	£9.99	Falmouth	1-85937-066-7	£12.99
Carmarthenshire	1-85937-216-3	£14.99	Folkestone (pb)	1-85937-124-8	£9.99
Chelmsford (pb)	1-85937-310-0	£9.99	Glasgow (pb)	1-85937-190-6	£9.99
Cheltenham (pb)	1-85937-095-0	£9.99	Gloucestershire	1-85937-102-7	£14.99
Cheshire (pb)	1-85937-271-6	£9.99	Great Yarmouth (pb)	1-85937-426-3	£9.99
Chester	1-85937-090-x	£12.99	Greater Manchester (pb)	1-85937-266-x	£9.99
Chesterfield	1-85937-378-x	£9.99	Guildford (pb)	1-85937-410-7	£9.99
Chichester (pb)	1-85937-228-7	£9.99	Hampshire (pb)	1-85937-279-1	£9.99
Colchester (pb)	1-85937-188-4	£8.99	Hampshire Churches (pb)	1-85937-207-4	£9.99
Cornish Coast	1-85937-163-9	£14.99	Harrogate	1-85937-423-9	£9.99
Cornwall (pb)	1-85937-229-5	£9.99	Hastings & Bexhill (pb)	1-85937-131-0	£9.99
Cornwall Living Memories	1-85937-248-1	£14.99	Heart of Lancashire (pb)	1-85937-197-3	£9.99
Cotswolds (pb)	1-85937-230-9	£9.99	Helston (pb)	1-85937-214-7	£9.99
Cotswolds Living Memories	1-85937-255-4	£14.99	Hereford (pb)	1-85937-175-2	£9.99
County Durham	1-85937-123-x	£14.99	Herefordshire	1-85937-174-4	£14.99
Croydon Living Memories	1-85937-162-0	£9.99	Hertfordshire (pb)	1-85937-247-3	£9.99
Cumbria	1-85937-101-9	£14.99	Horsham (pb)	1-85937-432-8	£9.99
Dartmoor	1-85937-145-0	£14.99	Humberside	1-85937-215-5	£14.99
			Hythe, Romney Marsh & Ashford	1-85937-256-2	£9.99

Available from your local bookshop or from the publisher

Frith Book Co Titles (continued)

Ipswich (pb)	1-85937-424-7	£9.99	St Ives (pb)	1-85937415-8	£9.99
Ireland (pb)	1-85937-181-7	£9.99	Scotland (pb)	1-85937-182-5	£9.99
Isle of Man (pb)	1-85937-268-6	£9.99	Scottish Castles (pb)	1-85937-323-2	£9.99
Isles of Scilly	1-85937-136-1	£14.99	Sevenoaks & Tunbridge	1-85937-057-8	£12.99
Isle of Wight (pb)	1-85937-429-8	£9.99	Sheffield, South Yorks (pb)	1-85937-267-8	£9.99
Isle of Wight Living Memories	1-85937-304-6	£14.99	Shrewsbury (pb)	1-85937-325-9	£9.99
Kent (pb)	1-85937-189-2	£9.99	Shropshire (pb)	1-85937-326-7	£9.99
Kent Living Memories	1-85937-125-6	£14.99	Somerset	1-85937-153-1	£14.99
Lake District (pb)	1-85937-275-9	£9.99	South Devon Coast	1-85937-107-8	£14.99
Lancaster, Morecambe & Heysham (pb)	1-85937-233-3	£9.99	South Devon Living Memories	1-85937-168-x	£14.99
Leeds (pb)	1-85937-202-3	£9.99	South Hams	1-85937-220-1	£14.99
Leicester	1-85937-073-x	£12.99	Southampton (pb)	1-85937-427-1	£9.99
Leicestershire (pb)	1-85937-185-x	£9.99	Southport (pb)	1-85937-425-5	£9.99
Lincolnshire (pb)	1-85937-433-6	£9.99	Staffordshire	1-85937-047-0	£12.99
Liverpool & Merseyside (pb)	1-85937-234-1	£9.99	Stratford upon Avon	1-85937-098-5	£12.99
London (pb)	1-85937-183-3	£9.99	Suffolk (pb)	1-85937-221-x	£9.99
Ludlow (pb)	1-85937-176-0	£9.99	Suffolk Coast	1-85937-259-7	£14.99
Luton (pb)	1-85937-235-x	£9.99	Surrey (pb)	1-85937-240-6	£9.99
Maidstone	1-85937-056-x	£14.99	Sussex (pb)	1-85937-184-1	£9.99
Manchester (pb)	1-85937-198-1	£9.99	Swansea (pb)	1-85937-167-1	£9.99
Middlesex	1-85937-158-2	£14.99	Tees Valley & Cleveland	1-85937-211-2	£14.99
New Forest	1-85937-128-0	£14.99	Thanet (pb)	1-85937-116-7	£9.99
Newark (pb)	1-85937-366-6	£9.99	Tiverton (pb)	1-85937-178-7	£9.99
Newport, Wales (pb)	1-85937-258-9	£9.99	Torbay	1-85937-063-2	£12.99
Newquay (pb)	1-85937-421-2	£9.99	Truro	1-85937-147-7	£12.99
Norfolk (pb)	1-85937-195-7	£9.99	Victorian and Edwardian Cornwall	1-85937-252-x	£14.99
Norfolk Living Memories	1-85937-217-1	£14.99	Victorian & Edwardian Devon	1-85937-253-8	£14.99
Northamptonshire	1-85937-150-7	£14.99	Victorian & Edwardian Kent	1-85937-149-3	£14.99
Northumberland Tyne & Wear (pb)	1-85937-281-3	£9.99	Vic & Ed Maritime Album	1-85937-144-2	£17.99
North Devon Coast	1-85937-146-9	£14.99	Victorian and Edwardian Sussex	1-85937-157-4	£14.99
North Devon Living Memories	1-85937-261-9	£14.99	Victorian & Edwardian Yorkshire	1-85937-154-x	£14.99
North London	1-85937-206-6	£14.99	Victorian Seaside	1-85937-159-0	£17.99
North Wales (pb)	1-85937-298-8	£9.99	Villages of Devon (pb)	1-85937-293-7	£9.99
North Yorkshire (pb)	1-85937-236-8	£9.99	Villages of Kent (pb)	1-85937-294-5	£9.99
Norwich (pb)	1-85937-194-9	£8.99	Villages of Sussex (pb)	1-85937-295-3	£9.99
Nottingham (pb)	1-85937-324-0	£9.99	Warwickshire (pb)	1-85937-203-1	£9.99
Nottinghamshire (pb)	1-85937-187-6	£9.99	Welsh Castles (pb)	1-85937-322-4	£9.99
Oxford (pb)	1-85937-411-5	£9.99	West Midlands (pb)	1-85937-289-9	£9.99
Oxfordshire (pb)	1-85937-430-1	£9.99	West Sussex	1-85937-148-5	£14.99
Peak District (pb)	1-85937-280-5	£9.99	West Yorkshire (pb)	1-85937-201-5	£9.99
Penzance	1-85937-069-1	£12.99	Weymouth (pb)	1-85937-209-0	£9.99
Peterborough (pb)	1-85937-219-8	£9.99	Wiltshire (pb)	1-85937-277-5	£9.99
Piers	1-85937-237-6	£17.99	Wiltshire Churches (pb)	1-85937-171-x	£9.99
Plymouth	1-85937-119-1	£12.99	Wiltshire Living Memories	1-85937-245-7	£14.99
Poole & Sandbanks (pb)	1-85937-251-1	£9.99	Winchester (pb)	1-85937-428-x	£9.99
Preston (pb)	1-85937-212-0	£9.99	Windmills & Watermills	1-85937-242-2	£17.99
Reading (pb)	1-85937-238-4	£9.99	Worcester (pb)	1-85937-165-5	£9.99
Romford (pb)	1-85937-319-4	£9.99	Worcestershire	1-85937-152-3	£14.99
Salisbury (pb)	1-85937-239-2	£9.99	York (pb)	1-85937-199-x	£9.99
Scarborough (pb)	1-85937-379-8	£9.99	Yorkshire (pb)	1-85937-186-8	£9.99
St Albans (pb)	1-85937-341-0	£9.99	Yorkshire Living Memories	1-85937-166-3	£14.99

See Frith books on the internet www.francisfrith.co.uk

FRITH PRODUCTS & SERVICES

Francis Frith would doubtless be pleased to know that the pioneering publishing venture he started in 1860 still continues today. A hundred and forty years later, The Francis Frith Collection continues in the same innovative tradition and is now one of the foremost publishers of vintage photographs in the world. Some of the current activities include:

Interior Decoration

Today Frith's photographs can be seen framed and as giant wall murals in thousands of pubs, restaurants, hotels, banks, retail stores and other public buildings throughout the country. In every case they enhance the unique local atmosphere of the places they depict and provide reminders of gentler days in an increasingly busy and frenetic world.

Product Promotions

Frith products are used by many major companies to promote the sales of their own products or to reinforce their own history and heritage. Frith promotions have been used by Hovis bread, Courage beers, Scots Porage Oats, Colman's mustard, Cadbury's foods, Mellow Birds coffee, Dunhill pipe tobacco, Guinness, and Bulmer's Cider.

Genealogy and Family History

As the interest in family history and roots grows world-wide, more and more people are turning to Frith's photographs of Great Britain for images of the towns, villages and streets where their ancestors lived; and, of course, photographs of the churches and chapels where their ancestors were christened, married and buried are an essential part of every genealogy tree and family album.

Frith Products

All Frith photographs are available Framed or just as Mounted Prints and Posters (size 23 x 16 inches). These may be ordered from the address below. From time to time other products - Address Books, Calendars, Table Mats, etc - are available.

The Internet

Already twenty thousand Frith photographs can be viewed and purchased on the internet through the Frith websites and a myriad of partner sites.

For more detailed information on Frith companies and products, look at these sites:

www.francisfrith.co.uk
www.francisfrith.com
(for North American visitors)

See the complete list of Frith Books at:

www.francisfrith.co.uk

This web site is regularly updated with the latest list of publications from the Frith Book Company. If you wish to buy books relating to another part of the country that your local bookshop does not stock, you may purchase on-line.

For further information, trade, or author enquiries please contact us at the address below:
The Francis Frith Collection, Frith's Barn, Teffont, Salisbury, Wiltshire, England SP3 5QP.
Tel: +44 (0)1722 716 376 Fax: +44 (0)1722 716 881 Email: sales@francisfrith.co.uk

---

See Frith books on the internet www.francisfrith.co.uk

TO RECEIVE YOUR **FREE** MOUNTED PRINT

Mounted Print
Overall size 14 x 11 inches

Cut out this Voucher and return it with your remittance for £1.95 to cover postage and handling, to UK addresses. For overseas addresses please include £4.00 post and handling. Choose any photograph included in this book. Your SEPIA print will be A4 in size, and mounted in a cream mount with burgundy rule line, overall size 14 x 11 inches.

Order additional Mounted Prints at HALF PRICE (only £7.49 each*)

If there are further pictures you would like to order, possibly as gifts for friends and family, purchase them at half price (no additional postage and handling required).

Have your Mounted Prints framed*

For an additional £14.95 per print you can have your chosen Mounted Print framed in an elegant polished wood and gilt moulding, overall size 16 x 13 inches (no additional postage and handling required).

---

* IMPORTANT!
These special prices are only available if ordered using the original voucher on this page (no copies permitted) and at the same time as your free Mounted Print, for delivery to the same address

---

Frith Collectors' Guild

From time to time we publish a magazine of news and stories about Frith photographs and further special offers of Frith products. If you would like 12 months FREE membership, please return this form.

Send completed forms to:
The Francis Frith Collection, Frith's Barn, Teffont, Salisbury, Wiltshire SP3 5QP

Voucher for **FREE** and Reduced Price Frith Prints

Picture no.	Page number	Qty	Mounted @ £7.49	Framed + £14.95	Total Cost
		1	**Free of charge***	£	£
			£7.49	£	£
			£7.49	£	£
			£7.49	£	£
			£7.49	£	£
			£7.49	£	£

Please allow 28 days for delivery	*** Post & handling**	**£1.95**
Book Title	**Total Order Cost**	**£**

Please do not photocopy this voucher. Only the original is valid, so please cut it out and return it to us.

I enclose a cheque / postal order for £ . . . .
made payable to 'The Francis Frith Collection'
OR please debit my Mastercard / Visa / Switch / Amex card
(credit cards please on all overseas orders)

Number . . . .

Issue No(Switch only) . . . . .Valid from (Amex/Switch) . . . .

Expires . . . . Signature . . . .

Name Mr/Mrs/Ms . . . .

Address . . . .

. . . .

. . . .

. . . . Postcode . . . .

Daytime Tel No . . . .   Valid to 31/12/03

The Francis Frith Collectors' Guild
Please enrol me as a member for 12 months free of charge.

Name Mr/Mrs/Ms . . . .

Address . . . .

. . . .

. . . .

. . . . Postcode . . . .

Would you like to find out more about Francis Frith?

We have recently recruited some entertaining speakers who are happy to visit local groups, clubs and societies to give an illustrated talk documenting Frith's travels and photographs. If you are a member of such a group and are interested in hosting a presentation, we would love to hear from you.

Our speakers bring with them a small selection of our local town and county books, together with sample prints. They are happy to take orders. A small proportion of the order value is donated to the group who have hosted the presentation. The talks are therefore an excellent way of fundraising for small groups and societies.

Can you help us with information about any of the Frith photographs in this book?

We are gradually compiling an historical record for each of the photographs in the Frith archive. It is always fascinating to find out the names of the people shown in the pictures, as well as insights into the shops, buildings and other features depicted.

If you recognize anyone in the photographs in this book, or if you have information not already included in the author's caption, do let us know. We would love to hear from you, and will try to publish it in future books or articles.

Our production team

Frith books are produced by a small dedicated team at offices in the converted Grade II listed 18th-century barn at Teffont near Salisbury, illustrated above. Most have worked with the Frith Collection for many years. All have in common one quality: they have a passion for the Frith Collection. The team is constantly expanding, but currently includes:

Jason Buck, John Buck, Douglas Burns, Heather Crisp, Lucy Elcock, Isobel Hall, Rob Hames, Hazel Heaton, Peter Horne, James Kinnear, Tina Leary, Hannah Marsh, Eliza Sackett, Terence Sackett, Sandra Sanger, Lewis Taylor, Shelley Tolcher, Helen Vimpany, Clive Wathen and Jenny Wathen.